Ten Poe
about Fatners

ex libris

Candlestick Press

Published by:

Candlestick Press,
Diversity House, 72 Nottingham Road, Arnold, Nottingham NG5 6LF
www.candlestickpress.co.uk

Design and typesetting by Craig Twigg

Printed by Ratcliff & Roper Print Group, Nottinghamshire, UK

Introduction © Di Slaney, 2012

Cover illustration © Carol Walklin, 2012

Candlestick Press monogram © Barbara Shaw, 2008

© Candlestick Press, 2012
Reprinted 2013, 2014
Updated 2019
Reprinted 2022

ISBN: 978 1 907598 12 8

Dedicated to David George Spencer, dad of distinction.

Acknowledgements:

Candlestick Press thanks Jacek Laskowski for his help in researching these
poems. Our thanks to Tony Harrison for permission to reprint 'Flood' from
Selected Poems (Penguin, 2006). 'Hot Food' by Michael Rosen from *The
Hypnotiser* (© Michael Rosen, 1988) is reproduced by permission of United
Agents (www.unitedagents.co.uk) on behalf of Michael Rosen; 'Snow' by
Louise Glück is reproduced from *The First Five Books of Poems* (Carcanet
Press, 1997); 'Marks of Time' by Coral Bracho is reproduced by permission of
the Poetry Translation Centre from Coral Bracho, *Poems* (Enitharmon Press/
Poetry Translation Centre, 2008). © Coral Bracho 2008, translation from
the Spanish © Katherine Pierpoint and Tom Boll. More of Coral Bracho's
poems in translation can be read on the Poetry Translation Centre's website,
www.poetrytranslation.org. 'The Return' by Joanne Limburg first appeared
in *Femenismo* (Bloodaxe Books, 2000); 'A Harvest of Wheat' by Tariq Latif
is reprinted from *The Minister's Garden* (Arc Publications, 1996); 'Cinders'
by Roger McGough originally appeared in *Defying Gravity* (Penguin, 1993).
Thanks are also due to the following for their kind permission: Shazea
Quraishi, *The Art of Scratching* (Bloodaxe Books, 2015) www.bloodaxebooks.
com. Siriol Troup, *No Names Have Been Changed* (Shearsman Books, 2017) by
kind permission of the author and publisher.

Where poets are no longer living, their dates are given.

Introduction

Everyone's relationship with their father is different, even those whose relationship is in absentia. These poems are an introduction to the many brilliant poems written about fathers and fatherhood. Some of these poems are about the writer's father; others are about the experience of fatherhood. Some are about both.

My own dear dad is a man of few words, and very little sentiment. We were recently looking at a photo that he'd taken of me as a baby: cherubic infant, hair all spiked up, being bathed in the kitchen sink. I expected some comment about how lovely I was when I was little, only to hear the words "Do you know, I'd forgotten how good that sink was – they don't make them like that anymore". But his camera told a different story, and I've never doubted for a moment how much he loves me, without him ever having to say it. There are several poems in this small selection about that unspoken bond of affection between father and child, and how it often manifests in curious ways.

I know many a dad will appreciate the practical, plain-speaking father in Tony Harrison's 'Flood', and his preoccupation with plumbing matters. I suspect they'll also like the potato-stuffing dad in 'Hot Food' by Michael Rosen (my own father's party trick was to pop three whole digestive biscuits into his mouth at the same time).

Everyone's dad is unique: we hope that this pamphlet portrays a realistic mixture of good and bad dads, and the people who loved them enough to write about them.

Di Slaney

Snow

Late December: my father and I
are going to New York, to the circus.
He holds me
on his shoulders in the bitter wind:
scraps of white paper
blow over the railroad ties.

My father liked
to stand like this, to hold me
so he couldn't see me.
I remember
staring straight ahead
into the world my father saw;
I was learning
to absorb its emptiness,
the heavy snow
not falling, whirling around us.

Louise Glück

Cinders

After the pantomime, carrying you back to the car
On the coldest night of the year
My coat, black leather, cracking in the wind.

Through the darkness we are guided by a star
It is the one the Good Fairy gave you
You clutch it tightly, your magic wand.

And I clutch you tightly for fear you blow away
For fear you grow up too soon and – suddenly,
I almost slip, so take it steady down the hill.

Hunched against the wind and hobbling
I could be mistaken for your grandfather
And sensing this, I hold you tighter still.

Knowing that I will never see you dressed for the Ball
Be on hand to warn you against Prince Charmings
And the happy ever afters of pantomime.

On reaching the car I put you into the baby seat
And fumble with straps I have yet to master
Thinking, if only there were more time. More time.

You are crying now. Where is your wand?
Oh no. I can't face going back for it
Let some kid find it in tomorrow's snow.

Waiting in the wings, the witching hour.
Already the car is changing. Smells sweet
Of ripening seed. We must go. Must go.

Roger McGough

You May Have Heard of Me

My father was a bear.
He carried me through forest, sky
and over frozen sea. At night
I lay along his back
wrapped in fur and heat
and while I slept, he ran,
never stopping to rest, never
letting me fall.
He showed me how to be careful as stone
sharp as thorn and quick
as weather. When he hunted alone
he'd leave me somewhere safe – high up a tree
or deep within a cave.
And then a day went on...
He didn't come.
I looked and looked for him.
The seasons changed and changed again.
Sleep became my friend. It even brought my father back.
The dark was like his fur,
the sea's breathing echoed his breathing.
I left home behind, an empty skin.
Alone, I walked taller, balanced better.
So I came to the gates of this city
– tall, black gates with teeth.
Here you find me, keeping my mouth small,
hiding pointed teeth and telling stories,
concealing their truth as I conceal
the thick black fur on my back.

Shazea Quraishi

Father William

"You are old, Father William," the young man said,
"And your hair has become very white;
And yet you incessantly stand on your head –
Do you think, at your age, it is right?"

"In my youth," Father William replied to his son,
"I feared it might injure the brain;
But, now that I'm perfectly sure I have none,
Why, I do it again and again."

"You are old," said the youth, "as I mentioned before,
And have grown most uncommonly fat;
Yet you turned a back-somersault in at the door –
Pray, what is the reason of that?"

"In my youth," said the sage, as he shook his grey locks,
"I kept all my limbs very supple
By the use of this ointment – one shilling the box –
Allow me to sell you a couple?"

"You are old," said the youth, "and your jaws are too weak
For anything tougher than suet;
Yet you finished the goose, with the bones and the beak –
Pray how did you manage to do it?"

"In my youth," said his father, "I took to the law,
And argued each case with my wife;
And the muscular strength which it gave to my jaw,
Has lasted the rest of my life."

"You are old," said the youth, "one would hardly suppose
That your eye was as steady as ever;
Yet you balanced an eel on the end of your nose –
What made you so awfully clever?"

"I have answered three questions, and that is enough,"
Said his father, "don't give yourself airs!
Do you think I can listen all day to such stuff?
Be off, or I'll kick you down stairs!"

Lewis Carroll (1832 – 1898)

Flood

His home address was inked inside his cap
and on every piece of paper that he carried
even across the church porch of the snap
that showed him with mi mam just minutes married.

But if ah'm found at 'ome (he meant found dead)
turn t'water off. Through his last years he nursed,
more than a fear of dying, a deep dread
of his last bath running over, or a burst.

Each night towards the end he'd pull the flush
then wash, then in pyjamas, rain or snow,
go outside, kneel down in the yard, and push
the stopcock as far off as it would go.

For though hoping that he'd drop off in his sleep
he was most afraid, I think, of not being 'found'
there in their house, his ark, on firm Leeds ground
but somewhere that kept moving, cold, dark, deep.

Tony Harrison

Hot Food

We sit down to eat
and the potato's a bit hot
so I only put a little bit on my fork
and I blow
whooph whooph
until it's cool
just cool
then into the mouth
nice.
And there's my brother
he's doing the same
whooph whooph
into the mouth
nice.
There's my mum
she's doing the same
whooph whooph
into the mouth
nice.
But my dad.
My dad.
What does he do?
He stuffs a great big chunk of potato
into his mouth.
Then
that really does it.
His eyes pop out
he flaps his hands
he blows, he puffs, he yells
he bobs his head up and down
he spits bits of potato
all over his plate
and he turns to us and he says,
'Watch out everybody –
the potato's very hot.'

Michael Rosen

The Return

Dad,
I come home
and find you sitting
in every room in the house,
its smell your smell,
as if it were a jacket
you'd only just thrown off,
still warm.

As the house recalls you,
so do I,
resurrecting you
fifty times a day,
in the way you clench my teeth
when something fails to work,
as we prowl in step together
round my room,
hours into the night,
as you fret me into being ready
an hour early for every journey.
As I bite into something undercooked,
I feel you pull
that comical, disappointed face.

You prefer to hide
in better foods:
strong cheese, strong coffee,
anything sweet.
I find myself eating
a whole quarter of wine gums
just to give you
twenty more minutes
of borrowed life.

Joanne Limburg

My father plans to meet me on the other side

He's been meeting me for years:
stations, airports, docks,
Kuwait, Berlin, Benghazi, a field once
near Maastricht, full of startled cows.

His shadow through glass.
His smile opening doors and duty-free.
His half-salute –
four fingers and a stump of thumb.

And time cracking the tarmac
like phantoms or harriers.

His faith is everlasting:
Queen and Regiment, the BBC,
the healing powers of cabbage-water,
David Niven's heaven.

I know the form:
he'll pace the halls and check
the empty gates, holding his breath,
tapping his walnut stick,

praying I'll change the ending
where he waits and waits.

Siriol Troup

A Harvest of Wheat

All day the sounds of scythes
Cutting stalks. Our hands sticky
With juices, our arms heavy
With swathes of wheat.

All day in the blazing sun.
Our backs arched, eyes focused
On the sharp blade and the stems.
Slicing and gathering systematically.

All day in a kind of communion:
My father reciting the Koran;
My brothers and cousins and nephews
Exchanging stories and jokes. Our lives

Inter-mingling, growing around words.
Above us, the crows caw all day.
By evening there are bales of wheat
Scattered in an open field.

The women near the edges make
Nan bread. The scent of dough,
Baking, comforts our exhausted bodies.
Embers float up into the navy sky.

One by one stars begin to glimmer.
We navigate ourselves towards Mecca.
My father's voice rises between us.
His words crumble in my mouth.

Tariq Latif

Marks of Time

Between wind and dark,
between a rush of joy
yet deepest calm,
between my lovely white dress flying
and the dark, dark hole of the mine,
are my father's eyes, so gentle, waiting; his dancing
happiness. I go to meet him. This is a land
of little stars, of pyrite crystals,
wherever it's touched by the sunset. Clouds
of quartz, and flint, up high. His bright gaze,
all-embracing,
has the warmth of amber.
He lifts me up into his arms. He comes in close.
Our one shadow drifts over to the edge of the mine. He puts me down.
He gives me his hand.
The whole way down
is just one joy, in silence:
one dark warmth,
one richness, aglow.
Something in that quietness holds us under its wing, it protects
and uplifts us,
very softly,
as we go down.

Coral Bracho, trans. Tom Boll and Katherine Pierpoint